I AM LEAH

When You are Sick and Tired
&
Need a Right Now Praise

I AM LEAH

When You are Sick and Tired
&
Need a Right Now Praise

CYNTHIA ROBINSON

Seeing Is Believing

WHOLE WITHOUT A CRACK
PUBLICATIONS

I AM LEAH

When You are Sick and Tired
&
Need a Right Now Praise

Copyright © 2012 by Cynthia Robinson
Cover by Angel Prints
Author Photograph by Minnie Moore

All rights reserved. No part of this book may be reproduced in any form by any electronic or mechanical means including photocopying, recording, or information storage and retrieval without permission in writing from the author.

ISBN: 978-0-9834095-5-7

Book Website:
www.iamleah.org
Email: cyntrob01@yahoo.com

Printed by Whole Without A Crack Publications
www.wwacpselfpublishing.net
Printed in U.S.A.

Acknowledgements

I would like to thank everyone that has helped one way or another in my walk with Christ. I know I cannot write everyone's name, but I thank you all just the same. There are some people I must acknowledge. To my wonderful husband who has the patience of Job and the temperament of Peter, I love you. To my kids I love you all. To my first Pastor Bishop Tubbs and Sister Tubbs for teaching me the true word of God: thank you for praying for me when I would not listen to guidance. To my Shepherd, Pastor Barbara Glanton of the Love of Jesus Family Church of Newark: thank you for being a wonderful woman of God. To Pastor Jason Alvarez, the Pastor of Love of Jesus Family Church in Orange: I have learned from you to have a better bible study life. Your ministry has allowed different women and men of God to grace your pulpit. You have taught the fivefold ministry and strengthened the servants of God. To the following Pastors who have encouraged and enlightened this process: Pastor Brackett, Co-Pastor Crenshaw, Bishop Gerard Lloyd, Pastor Fred, Pastor Capers, Joyce Myers, Beth Moore and always to my spiritual as well as my biological mother, Dr. Ann Kidd. I love you and thank you for showing and making me the woman I am. I must thank the one the true and living God. He is worth all the praise, glory and honor. I love my father, my husband Jesus and the Holy Spirit that is with me always.

Contents

Acknowledgements...5
Dedication...8
Prelude to the Journey...9

Chapter 1 - The two sisters....................11
    What is your name?..........................13
    What did you say?...........................15
    Grown-up..18
    Our new family................................20

Chapter 2 - We are married..................23
    Will he work for you?.......................26
    Who am I married to?......................30
    The Princess and the Prostitute.........32
    Now I will marry my wife..................35

Chapter 3 - I am afflicted in my house...37
    What is my name mommy?...............39
    He has seen my affliction..................40
    We are not alone in our affliction......40
    He will love me now..........................41

Chapter 4 - I am hated in this house......43
    My sister wife hates me.....................45
    My husband hates me........................46
    God hears you...................................46
    I need freedom..................................48

Chapter 5 - I need a companion............51

Who's child are you?......................................53
I will take care of it for you?..........................54
How do I look?..55
The Devil..57
Jesus...62

Chapter 6 - I have my praise..................69
I have a testimony..71
Come on and Praise him..............................72

Epilogue..79
Prayers for God's Daughters.................83

Dedication

I am dedicating this book to the memory of my sister Melvina Kidd. Mel, I wish I know better so that I would have done better to help you get better. I will be a better sister to all my sisters in your memory.

Prelude to the Journey

A destination is the ultimate purpose for which something is created or intended (1).

We all have a destination which we have to get to. It is the reason we were created. The destination is determined by the journey we take. The journey will be difficult at times. We will have valleys, mountains and wilderness experiences we will have to go through. We will be separated from some people, places and things. They will not add, but be a distraction on the journey. Jesus was very clear about the journey and what we should have. Mark 6:8 he commanded ***"And commanded them that they should take nothing for their journey, save a staff only; no scrip, no bread, no money in their purse:***

We are on a journey that has already prepared for us. This trip is new to us, but not to God. He has given us all we need. We do not need a script (reading material), bread (earthly food) or money (cash or power). Jesus will provide for us along the way.

Our destination may seem unclear sometimes. It may seem like everything is upside down and we do not know which way is up. It may seem like we will not make it over the mountains, through the valleys and out of the wilderness. Let me reassure you that you will make it. Our heavenly Father has not forsaken us neither will he just leaves us here alone to be Satan's play toys.

***Deut. 31:6** "Be strong and of a good courage, fear not, nor be afraid of them: for the LORD thy God, he it is that doth go with thee; he will not fail thee, nor forsake thee."*

God has a destination planned out for us. If we follow his instructions, we will get there. I cannot and will not say what your destination is, but I can say we are all traveling down this road and if we all hear God's, instruction it leads to heaven.

1

The Two Sisters

Genesis 29:16-17

"And Laban Had Two Daughters: The Name Of The Elder Was Leah, And The Name Of The Younger Was Rachel."

"Leah Was Tender Eyed; But Rachel Was Beautiful And Well Favoured."

THE TWO SISTERS

The two daughters of Laban, Leah and Rachel, are two of the most dynamic, controversial and complex women in the Old Testament. Their journey starts in the book of Genesis, chapter 29. We are introduced to these two women who will give God something so special. They are the mother's of the children of Israel.

Rachel and Leah were two sisters who grew up together. They lived in the same house with the same father and mother. They had the same brothers, sisters and friends. However, their outlooks on their lives were completely different.

They are both biological and spiritual sisters. Each knew God and served him. Leah serves God more so than Rachel (Gen.31:19). Leah is described as the tender eyed one and Rachel as beautiful and well favored. It is important to understand why their names played a major role in their lives.

What is your name?

In biblical times your name was very important. There was meaning behind it. Your name could have been a symbol of a family name to prolong the legacy of your people. It can also represent something special that happened before, during or after your birth. It could even be that you have a birth defect or difference in your appearance.

Leah's name means weary or tired eye. The true meaning of her name is still in debate to this day. Some believe that it could mean she had a lazy eye. Others believed her eye color was not the color of the culture (just like today blues eyes are considered the eye color of beauty). Whether she had a birth defect or just a different eye color, she was a problem for her father. Leah was labeled a burden. Her father was faced with the possibility that Leah would be with him for the rest of her life. She would never have a husband, a family of her own or any type of future to think of. As cruel as this may seem it is the truth. Leah did not stand a chance.

Her sister, Rachel, on the other hand, was a different story. Her name meant ewe, lamb, sheep or purity. She would be the one to get married, have a family and a future. She is the one who will be favored because she is beautiful. Rachel's father would be free of her knowing she would be properly taken care of. Her father did not worry about her. Laban knew that the dowry he would get for Rachel would be great. Rachel was liked and favored by men because of her beauty.

How our families name us can literally be the death of us. We may not have been named as Leah and Rachel were, but we are named by our families. They name us by using negative words to describe us. They use the power in their tongues. Psalms 18:21 says, **"Death and life are in the power of the tongue."** Our family either blesses us or curses us. They either love us or hate us. We either are a helper or a hindrance to them. Our families can really damage us. They say and do some of the most harmful things to us. This not just in our families, but it is a common occurrence throughout the bible. We come by it naturally. Our forefathers and fore mothers started it. The following families have played major role in the shaping of our natural (fleshly) family history:

Adam and Eve- The first husband and wife to disobey God with deadly consequences - Genesis 2:16-17

Cain and Abel- sibling rival that went way too far- Genesis 4:1-9

Abram and Sarai- Husband and wife only when it meant no death to him because she was so beautiful- Genesis 12:14-20; - Genesis 20:1-13

Sarai and Hagar- the first co-wives that spelled destruction - Genesis 16:1-6

There are countless other examples of such things in the bible. We can even look into our own families to find get real time examples of how the words of family members shape us.

What did you say!!!

PROVERBS 26:22

The words of a talebearer are as wounds, and they go down into the innermost parts of the belly.

A talebearer is one who spreads gossip or rumors (2).

Leah had her share of talebearers in her family. They were openly talking about Leah's looks. They cursed her and hurt her to the innermost parts of her being with their words. They gave her a bad outlook of herself. She was wounded by the very people that should have loved and supported her instead of talking about her. As with Leah, the same is true with us. We hear our family member's words being spoken over us. We later chew (listen) to them and subsequently we digest (accept) them. Their words become a part of us. They begin to shape who we are and how we feel about ourselves.

Have you ever noticed that you feel a certain way about yourself, but you don't know why? Maybe you do not like when people say you are pretty. This is because one of your family members has said something to you and it has given you a negative viewpoint about yourself. As a result, when people say you are pretty, you automatically say, "no I'm not." Your mind reflects back to the words spoken over you and they become truth. Sad to say most of us cannot accept praise, but will allow someone to say something negative towards us. We accept it as truth and internalize it and it produces a negative perception of us. Children who have parents who encourage them and not belittle them are the most blessed children.

Leah had the misfortune of growing up in a home where she was treated with little to no love. Her parents cursed her with her naming and probably continued as she grew up. She was told from birth that she was not attractive. This is a bad thing for a girl. Her mother is not mentioned, but I have to believe her mom was not much of a help for her daughter.

If you were blessed to have a good father and mother in your home, God bless you. Everyone was not as blessed. There is a major difference between being raised in a household where you do not feel loved, than in one where you are loved and nurtured. A two parent home has a good support system that works to help in raising their children. If one of the parents is not there, the other is. One of the parents may have been considered to be the primary caretaker, but there were still two parents available. You have a bread winner and the loving supporter. You had the joy of knowing that you have support all around you.

When you have a two-parent household where the parents are not happy, they have a tendency to visit their problems and concerns upon their children. They will argue openly with each other in front of the children and maybe even become physical. The children are then put in a position of being either a protector or neglectful. They either try to protect the mistreated parent by fighting the abusive parent or they may even stand in front of the abuser to block them from hitting the other parent. On the other hand, the child may actually find fault with the ill-treated parent and begin to abuse them verbally.

Single-parent households present a whole different set of problems. They may be a loving parent, but they are stretched thin. They have to be both the bread winner and loving supporter all in one. One parent has to be everything to everyone all at the same time (I was one of these). You try to compensate for the lack of the presence of the other parent or parents (You may be taking care of an immediate family member's child or made a guardian by the state). This type of household leaves gaps where a loving two-parent household traditionally does not.

You will miss certain areas of growth in a child's life because of your work schedule, other children or your own personal issues you are, or aren't, dealing with. Eventually it will lead to resentment by some children and/or rebellion from others during the teenage years. All children rebel, but a child who grows up in an abusive two or single-parent home tends to rebel sooner and/or more often.

Grown Up

As Leah grows up in her family, there becomes an obvious difference between herself and Rachel. There is no way of hiding or ignoring the difference in their looks. These differences shaped the way they thought about themselves and the world around them. Leah's imperfection has almost certainly made her shy and in all likelihood people teased her, but she either laughed or cried.

Sidebar: More than likely she cried.

As we begin to grow within the family, differences about us begin to emerge. You may have been the smart one. You pick up information fast. You were an honor roll student throughout your academic life. You became Ms. Smarty pants. You may be the flawless pretty one who has always had the privilege of receiving compliments even from complete strangers; you are Ms. Pretty. It may be that you have a wonderful sense of humor. You can crack a joke right off the top of your head. You have everyone in stitches with laughter; you are Ms. Jokester. These differences are what make us a part of the family.

Even with the best of families we still have people who have spoken things into our lives making us feel unloved. They make comments like:

"You know no one wants you that why you are have to live with me."

"You are just like you're no good ...." (You finish the statement)

"You are too light or too dark"

"You are too skinny or too fat"

"Your hair is too straight or too curly or too coarse" (kinky or nappy just keeping it real)

"If you were not here I would still be with her father.

The power of the tongue is something else! Proverbs 12:18 says, *"There is that speaketh like the piercings of a sword: but the tongue of the wise is health"*

As women, we get our image of how a woman should be

from the first lady of the house. This woman was your mother, aunt, grandmother, or stepmother. She is the first woman to show us how a woman should be treated. If our first female role model is loved, then she will show us love. If she is mistreated, she will mistreat her children or allow someone else to mistreat them. Were you blessed with a woman with a wise tongue or a sword? Or better yet is your tongue healthy?

Our New Family

For most of us the first enemy in our lives is our dysfunctional, neurotic, false witnessing, tale bearing family. They can and will destroy some of us if we let them. They have no vision for us and are unable to see our purpose. They have lived a cursed life because of the bad decisions they have made (choosing the wrong person to marry or to have children with and/or their wrong lifestyle). They have to live a life they hate and try to project their lives on to us. Thank God he will not allow this behavior forever. He truly loves us. We are not a burden to him. Once we accept Jesus as Our Lord, we are born into a new family. We are no longer an outsider.

In Romans 8:16-18 it is written,
[16]The Spirit itself beareth witness with our spirit, that we are the children of God:

[17]And if children, then heirs; heirs of God, and joint-heirs with Christ; if so be that we suffer with him, that we may be also glorified together.

[18]For I reckon that the sufferings of this present time are not worthy to be compared with the glory which shall be revealed in us.

As God's daughters our lives are not our own. We are joint heirs with Christ. The Holy Spirit bears witness with our spirit. We will not have to suffer through trials or tribulations alone. We have a comforter with us. The sufferings we go through do not and cannot compare or come in a close second place to the glory that shall be revealed in our lives. We will and can see the glory (beauty, power and honor) in God the Father, God the Son and God the Holy Spirit. We have a wonderful spiritual family and they have made provision for us.

2

We're Getting Married

Genesis 29:18-30

¹⁸And Jacob loved Rachel; and said, I will serve thee seven years for Rachel thy you Anger daughter.

¹⁹And Laban said, It is better that I give her to thee, than that I should give her to another man: abide with me.

²⁰And Jacob served seven years for Rachel; and they seemed unto him but a few days, for the love he had to her.

²¹And Jacob said unto Laban, Give me my wife, for my days are fulfilled, that I may go in unto her.
²²And Laban gathered together all the men of the place, and made a feast.

²³And it came to pass in the evening, that he took Leah his daughter, and brought her to him; and he went in unto her.

²⁴And Laban gave unto his daughter Leah Zilpah his maid for an handmaid.

²⁵And it came to pass, that in the morning, behold, it was Leah: and he said to Laban, What is this thou hast done unto me? Did not I serve with thee for Rachel? Wherefore then hast thou beguiled me?

²⁶And Laban said, It must not be so done in our country, to give the younger before the firstborn.

²⁷Fulfil her week, and we will give thee this also for the service which thou shalt serve with me yet seven other years.

²⁸And Jacob did so, and fulfilled her week: and he gave him Rachel his daughter to wife also.

²⁹And Laban gave to Rachel his daughter Bilhah his handmaid to be her maid.

³⁰And he went in also unto Rachel, and he loved also Rachel more than Leah, and served with him yet seven other years.

Leah has just been told that her younger and prettier sister is going to get married. Well, I'll be darned! Jacob just happens upon her at the well and now he is willing to work seven years in the field to have Rachel as his wife. Surely she thought they were kidding her. I always knew Leah was a spiritual woman, but I can only guess that her fleshly side had a few choice words about this, even if she never said them out loud. I know that if a man came to my father and said I will do your job for you for seven years only to have your daughter's hand in marriage, I would be in shock. This is a testament to the fact that a man is willing to do anything to get the woman he wants.

Sidebar: Let's stop right here.

Will he work for you?

There is an important subject matter to be addressed here. A man has to work for what he wants. The modern day woman doesn't quite understand the full scope of issue concerning men not wanting to work. A man needs to and has to work. This is not just some Old Testament writing and no, Christ's death and resurrection did not abolish it. Paul wrote in 2 Thess.3:10 it says, *"For even when we were with you, this we commanded you, that if any would not work, neither should he eat."*

Side bar- if you have a man in your life and he is not working, please do not yoke up with him. Let me explain a little further before you get mad.

WE ARE MARRIED

If you just met a man or you have a man in your life that you believe loves you and he has not worked in the past year or has never worked, there is a problem. If he isn't seriously looking for a job and is living at home with his parents or grandparents, watches television all day or plays Wii, Play Station or Xbox, run to the door and do not look back! Lot's wife looked back and you see what happened to her. We as women are always trying to nurture someone. We start with our family members, then our friends and eventually we turn these feeling to a man whom we believe has potential.

Side bar- a grown man does not have potential he just is who he is.

He is not going to change for you. You will only make him worse. He gives you excuses as to why he is not working. All of his excuses come from outside sources like the government, his mother, father, prison records and anything else he can think up to make you feel sorry for him. This is a lie from the pit of hell. Yes, some men who are ex-offenders have it a little harder than others, but if God be for him then who can be against him? You believe his excuses and feel sorry for him.

Sidebar: STOP THAT. He is a grown man.

You become yoked to him. The unequal yoke begins to choke you to death. Jacob was so in love with Rachel that he was ready to do anything to be with her. Jacob was willing to work toward his purpose. A man has to have a purpose. If you are the love of his life, then he will work to fulfill his purpose in your life. Jacob's love for Rachel would be his fuel for seven years. In verse 20 it says, **"and they seemed unto him but a few days for the love he had to her."** The love he had for her was so strong that it carried him through the years of hard labor.

Jacob was a mommy's boy who worked in the house. He did not do hard LABOR. His love for Rachel changed all that. He wanted her and there was nothing to stop him from getting her.

Stop right there. If a man is not willing to win you, then he is not worth you. I can testify to that.

I was brought up believing it is the man who takes care of the family. My father worked two jobs and my mother did not have to work. When she did choose to work her money was her money. She paid no bills in the house. My father told me, after my second child, that if I had to go on welfare, I needed to go by myself. It was the best advice my father ever gave me. It meant that if I had to go on welfare, don't support a man with my welfare money. It was for myself and my children. I remember one time I stopped seeing a guy because he asked me for five dollars. I do not support any man. My husband is different. The marriage is a covenant. We are united by God: man and woman and he (God) is the true provider for the both of us.

Men marry the women that motivate them, not the ones he can easily have. He will never respect you if you take care of him. He must take care of himself. Don't do it for him. When you act like his mother (do things for him that he should do for himself) don't get mad when he starts treating you like his mother. The man has to feel like he has a purpose. Jacob knows his purpose. His purpose was RACHEL. Does your man know his purpose? It should be you.

The bible says in Proverbs 18:22, ***"Who so findeth a wife findeth a good thing and obtaineth favor of the Lord."*** If you are a good find, why don't you let him look for you? Do not settle. God did not make us to settle. You are the apple of God's eye according to Deut 32:10. Why would you settle for the devil's messy seconds? A man who cannot and will not provide for you is not the man God says you should be with as the bible said. Yes, it is in the bible. After the fall of man God gave Adam clear instruction on how he is to take care of the woman Genesis 3:17-19:

[17]And unto Adam he said, Because thou hast hearkened unto the voice of thy wife, and hast eaten of the tree, of which I commanded thee, saying, Thou shalt not eat of it: cursed is the ground for thy sake; in sorrow shalt thou eat of it all the days of thy life;

[18]Thorns also and thistles shall it bring forth to thee; and thou shalt eat the herb of the field;

[19]In the sweat of thy face shalt thou eat bread, till thou return unto the ground; for out of it wast thou taken: for dust thou art, and unto dust shalt thou return.

The man is to work. If he does not work, he should not eat. The desire to work toward something has to be in him. Men need to and have to work toward the love of a woman. Men like that. We as women have a tendency to think we can make a man. We cannot make what we have never created. We did not create man so why do we try to make them into one? God created man and he knew how to make them. We have to allow God to raise his sons.

Sisters, we must learn to accept that God wants what is best for us. God has thought about us in ways we do not or cannot understand.

"For I know the thoughts that I think toward you, saith the LORD, thoughts of peace, and not of evil, to give you an expected end," Jeremiah 29:11.

What is the end you truly desire? Is it one with you as a faithful wife, married to a wonderful man who provides and supports you? Or does your end have you as a faithful wife who is married to a man whom you have to support and in return you receive nothing but abuse? You do not have to be yoked to the devil and living in hell.

Sidebar: BACK TO THE STORY

Who am I married to?

The devil is a busy little bee isn't he? Job 1:7 says, **"And the LORD said unto Satan, Whence comest thou?"** Then

WE ARE MARRIED

Satan answered the LORD, and said, **"From going to and fro in the earth, and from walking up and down in it."** Busy, busy, busy.

Jacob thought after those 7 years of hard work that he would go and get his wife. He approached Laban in verse 21 and told him to give him his wife. Jacob made it known that he had served his 7 years as promised and now it was time to collect his bride. Laban said sure son, but first let us celebrate. Laban made it seem as if he wanted to celebrate with the whole village concerning the marriage of his daughter.

Now, while Jacob is day dreaming about Rachel, Laban, her father, on the other hand, is scheming. He goes and gets Leah and tells her that she is to go into the marriage chamber with Jacob instead of Rachel. He plans to get Jacob drunk and knows the room will be so dark he won't be able to see it is Leah he's sleeping with until morning.

I am just guessing, but I believe Leah was both excited and upset. She was excited because she was finally getting married. She is the older sister. She is to be married first. Her dream would finally come true. On the other hand, she was upset because she is being put against her sister. Her younger sister who looked up to her was going to have her dreams destroyed. I believe Leah loved Rachel, but hated her too. She was envious of how her younger sister won the heart of Jacob and how he was willing to work seven years to have her. Please, I would have been jealous in much the same manner myself.

Leah could have ended the lie by simply opening her mouth and saying I am Leah. The moment Leah got into the bed and did not tell Jacob the truth was the moment she accepted her father's curse. Her father was a deceiver and now he has made her one. Don't get me wrong, I know Leah was put in a horrible place by her father, but the truth always weighs out a lie.

How many of us have generations after generations of curses we cannot seem to break. We cannot break them because they are our families' unspoken lies. Leah lay in that bed waiting for Jacob to love her. This is what she wanted. She had been around Jacob for seven years. He was working in the fields. They probably became good friends. I'm sure she was the liaison between Jacob and Rachel. Back then you did not talk to the person who was going to betroth you; He probably lived in the servant's quarters away from the family. Leah grows to know him and love him. Sisterly love maybe, but love nevertheless.

Their wonderful father saw his opportunity to unload his burden. He would push her off on him and then he won't have to wonder who will marry her.

The Princess and the Prostitute

The person who really makes us into a princess or a prostitute is our father. He can either be a good daddy who nurtures or a bad daddy who abuses or leaves us alone. The princess is the girl who is loved by her daddy and he will do anything for her. He will love her from birth. She is the apple of his eye. There is no one who is more important to him than his little girl. He loves her and in return, she loves him. She sees nothing short of god in front of her. He guides her, teaches her and chastises her when needed. He would never hurt her and will fight anyone who does. The love of this father is the same as the father in heaven. He loves us like this. He will not allow people to continuously hurt his daughter. A father will take revenge in due season.

The prostitute is the girl who has a father who was abusive or just not there for her. She looked for him, but he was not there for her. He is not happy about her birth and sees her as a burden instead of a blessing. He will not guide her, but mislead her. The prostitute's father will teach her things she should not know like how to smoke, drink, gamble, lie for him and may even have sex with her. He teaches her that she has no worth unless a dollar sign is attached to it. Her worth is always for sell. She believes she can buy love or that her love can be purchased. God does not love us like that. His love is unconditional and forever. God's love cannot be worked for or purchased. His love can only be accepted.

Laban pimped both of his daughters. He sold Leah for her sister's dowry. He destroyed Rachel's dreams for free labor. He should really get the worst dad of the year award.

It's the morning after and Jacob's reality is about hit him in the face. Jacob wakes up from a beautiful dream about making love to his pretty wife Rachel and was probably thinking about doing it again just in the daylight where he could see.

I AM LEAH

Side bar: I just believe this is how the situation went down.

Scene: Jacob awakened and sees Leah is in the bed and ACTION!

Jacob: "No, No this can't be Leah. What are you doing here!!!!! Where is my wife Rachel????? I didn't. No I can't have. I slept with Rachel not you right???"

Leah: "No, it was me Jacob. You slept with me last night. My father arranged it."

Jacob: "Where is your father!!!!!!! I need to see him NOW!!! This is some craziness."

And cut.

Oh the drama... Laban is a liar and a true son of Satan. He is full of deceitfulness. Laban's name means white. I do not know if that is because he was pale at birth or maybe there was leprosy around or during his birth. Leprosy back then meant unclean and he was definitely unclean. Jacob goes quickly to meet his father-in-law and ask some questions. "What is this that thou hast done to me?"

"Did I not work for Rachel?" "Why did you beguile me?"

Wait a minute let's go back. We need to recap a little about the history on our poor little Jacob. Jacob does not have clean hands. Did not Jacob have to run away from home because he was deceitful? Why yes, in Genesis 27 Jacob and his mother worked together to obtain his brother Esau's blessing from his ailing father. Jacob's name means deceiver. His name matches him doesn't it? Imagine someone tricking him out of what was supposed to be his. How the tables have turned against Jacob now. He is reaping what he sowed. We cannot sow hell and reap heaven.

Laban, the liar, knew that he had to stay cool. He calms Jacob down and cuts another deal that Rachel will be his wife in a week if he works another seven years. Isn't that a deal of a lifetime? Jacob not only got tricked into marrying the wrong daughter, but now he is being treated like fool in order to be with the woman he loves. He has to give seven more years of free labor to his uncle who has deceived him. The devil is a lair and the father thereof. Jacob, to say the least, is a little pissed. Here he was thinking how he was going to be out of debt to his uncle and will have his lovely wife and go home to his family (maybe). Now he is stuck with Leah and no Rachel for another week or even seven more years.

Now I will marry my wife

He had plans to marry Rachel, the woman of his dreams, not Leah, the nightmare he had the other night. Jacob was now unsure if he would have his wife. He had been told this story before and he was tricked into marrying Leah.

I AM LEAH

The end of the week comes and Jacob awaits the verdict. Rachel was dressed in her gown and Jacob in his suit. They waited so long for this day and now it is here (seven years and a week). They were married. I bet the first question Jacob asked was "Rachel is that you?" They have a night that seals their love for each other. Jacob had to work other seven years for his uncle but, to have Rachel it was worth it. Are you worth the wait? God believes so. God waits on us to come to him **"And therefore will the LORD wait, that he may be gracious unto you,"** Isaiah 30:18. He does not force us to receive him.

Rachel and Jacob are living the lives they have prayed for. But the sin in this home will cause God to look upon his daughters and set into motion a series of events that will make a nation for him.

3

I Am Afflicted In This House

Genesis 29:31-32

And when the LORD saw that Leah was hated, he opened her womb: but Rachel was barren.

And Leah conceived, and bare a son, and she called his name Reuben: for she said, Surely the LORD hath looked upon my affliction; now therefore my husband will love me.

I AM AFFLICTED IN MY HOUSE

Leah was in a bad place, but in perfect position. She was in a bad place because she was living in a house that was not her home. She was pawned off to her sister's husband as his wife. Then her sister turns around and marries the man. They are both so in love that it makes Leah feel unwelcomed in her own home. She is in this threesome that is so wrong on all levels. She is not loved by her husband and she is afflicted in this house. I mean her home. She is the first wife. Her sister cannot stand her and her husband probably only uses her when he cannot be with Rachel. This has to be for Leah a living hell. But God.

She was in the perfect position for God to bring a blessing. He sees her affliction and steps right in and blesses. Leah was blessed with a baby boy. In that culture and still today, to have a son is to know that you have an heir to the family legacy. God caused Rachel to be barren (just for a little while, she does have two children herself) so that Leah will have some love in this home. Leah was hurting and God knew how to take care of the pain. Leah's son was a healing point for her.

What is my name mommy?

The naming of her children will show where Leah's mindset was at the time of their births. We will take a closer look at each of the children names and what this means to Leah. The first son is Reuben.

Reuben- **1. Meaning he has seen affliction: 2. He will love me (3).**

Reuben's name has two-fold meaning. Her first son's name carries a lot of weight upon his little shoulders. He has a large burden. Most first born carried the burdens and/or joy of the family on their shoulders.

He has seen my affliction

God has seen her affliction. God has seen her trials. God has seen her suffering. God has seen her pain. Leah first acknowledges that her God has seen. She acknowledges that the God she serves has blessed her with a son. She acknowledges God being with her. The same God is with us. God sees all the trials, pains and suffering that we are going through. In Psalms 34:19 it says, ***"Many are the afflicted of the righteous: but the Lord delivers them out of them all. Not some or part of the way but out of them all."*** We do not serve a halfway God. He is a total deliverer. In Exodus 3:13-14, Moses asked God a question. We asked the same question to him constantly. What is your name? We are to paraphrase, "God who are you?" God said to Moses "I AM THAT I AM." God will be whatever you need him to be, however you need him to be, whenever you need to be and wherever you need him to be. He is the I AM. He is an ever present God. God does not leave his people alone.

We may not know which way to go, but God does and will lead us if we allow him. God does not push himself on us. He asks for entrance. God is a gentleman.

We are not alone in our afflictions.

Leah was not the first woman to be afflicted in her marriage. Hagar, Abram second wife or co-wife, was afflicted. Their story goes that Sarai suggested Abram marry Hagar in order to bring the child who God had promised them. He does and of course, she becomes pregnant. She becomes disrespectful to Sarai. Well, Sarai tells Abram about her and asks him to make her leave, Abram tells her to do it herself. After Sarai deals with Hagar, Hagar goes away. Our wonderful father God sends an angel to tell her to return and submit to Sarai. The angel tells her that the Lord heard her affliction and that he would bless her seed (Ishmael, which meaning God hears). This story sounds familiar doesn't it? Leah was afflicted like Hagar and God blessed her also. God does not and will not allow us to be afflicted always. God will send relief to us. God is constantly delivering us out of our afflictions.

He will love me

The problem with the birth of Reuben is that Leah does not really believe. Leah wants something from the birth of her son. Yes, God has blessed her with a child. She knows that Reuben is from God. However, there is still one little problem. Things have not changed. Jacob still does not love her the way he loves Rachel. She thought that the affliction would go away. She thought that the baby would help mend her damaged relationship with her sister Rachel and Jacob her husband would love her the way he loves Rachel.

As Leah did so, do we. We are trying to make a terrible

marriage (physical or mental abuse) or relationship work that is not going to. Leah was trying to make a dreadful situation better by having a baby. She did not realize that her problem was Jacob. Scripture states that when a man shall leaves his father and his mother that he shall cleave unto his wife (Gen.2:24). Jacob was not cleaving to his first wife. He was not treating Leah like a wife at all. He was treating her like she was nothing to him. God was not pleased. God is never pleased when we treat one another badly.

We need to understand that children cannot and should not be a way to help build a better marriage. This is not their job. It is the parents responsible to work on their own marriage. There has not been a baby born that brings harmony to an unhappy relationship. Yes, God saw her misery and blessed her with a child, but God did not intend for the baby to be love for the marriage. Leah was hoping that a baby would help the relationship between Jacob and herself.

Sidebar -*Leah was her divine self before her marriage to Jacob, but she turned into her fleshly self because she wanted what her sister had. The true love of a man.*

Having a baby doesn't make you his future wife. It just makes you his child's mother. To be the wife you must be loved by him first then the baby, not baby first then hope he will love you. That never works.

4

I Am Hated

Genesis 29:33

And she conceived again, and bare a son; and said, Because the LORD hath heard I was hated, he hath therefore given me this son also: and she called his name Simeon.

Leah's very being made her to be hated by her sister and husband. Hate is a strong word, but they really did despise her.

My sister wife hates me

If you read the scriptures, it says that God saw that Leah was hated and he opened her womb and made Rachel barren. The hatred between the sisters was so deep that God had to create a blessing for Leah. Rachel had her man and he had her. Leah was the unwanted wife who was just a burden to Jacob and the only one who would and could help her was her Heavenly father. He was watching out for Leah. In Jeremiah 31:28 The Lord says, **"And it shall come to pass, that like as I have watched over them, to pluck up, and to break down, and to throw down, and to destroy, and to afflict; so will I watch over them, to build, and to plant, saith the LORD."** Leah may have been hated in her home, but she was blessed of God. God was building something inside her that no one could see. We have that same God. He is building in us something no one can see. They see the natural, but there is a spirit that is growing and in due time it will come forth. In 1 Peter 2:4 it states, **"To whom coming, as unto living stone disallowed indeed of men, but chosen of God, and precious."** I love this scripture. Even when men try and throw us away, God comes and he calls us his chosen. This is not according to man or woman. It has nothing to do with how we look, talk, walk, or our family background, or our ethnicity. We are chosen of God because he knows us. He knows who we will be. In Jeremiah 1:5 God tells him something so important, **"Before I formed thee in the belly, I knew**

thee." God knows YOU, do not you ever forget it. God knew Leah and what her destination was. It may not have been an easy journey, but it was hers to take.

My husband hates me

Jacob, her husband who hates despises her, seems to have no problem sleeping with her. He seems to find his way to her room and keeping her pregnant. He may hate her because of the situation he is in. He was tricked into marrying her. If he did not marry her, he could have been released from his uncle. Jacob wanted to have just one wife and they would be living their lives liberated from all of this hard labor. Well, to be honest, it is not like Jacob could go home. Remember Jacob and his mother plotted and stole his brother's blessing from his father who was dying. His brother Esau was looking to hurt him. He was not much of a prize of a son was he? Now that he is being punked he is all upset. Poor Jacob! The old saying goes God do not like ugly is so true right now. Jacob's whole family was living under a generational curse of deception and lying. His mother is a liar and so is her brother. They have passed this curse to their children.

God hears you

Leah could not change the situation, but God, he heard her prayers. Do you know that God hears you? When people hurt you and you cry out to him He hears. That is Leah's second son's name. Simeon name means God hears or God heard. God will always hear his children cried. In Ps. 34:4 it says, **"I sought the**

LORD, and he heard me, and delivered me from all my fears."

Ps 34:6 **"This poor man cried and the LORD heard him, and saved him out of all his troubles."**

God will not ignore your cry, he hears them. He will come to our rescue. We do not serve a God who will leave us to suffer in this life. Know that God will come down for heaven on our behalf and fight our battles. In 2 Samuel 22:7-10 says:

7In my distress I called upon the LORD, and cried to my God: and he did hear my voice out of his temple, and my cry did enter into his ears.

8Then the earth shook and trembled; the foundations of heaven moved and shook, because he was wroth.

9There went up a smoke out of his nostrils, and fire out of his mouth devoured: coals were kindled by it.

10He bowed the heavens also, and came down; and darkness was under his feet.

These scriptures are about Gods favor upon us. He will bow the heavens and come down. God comes down or has come down and fought on the behalf of his people. I have never hear of Buddha, Allah or even Satan fighting for their people the way God fights for us.

Leah was in a house with no love. She was hated not only by her husband, but her sister too. Despite it all, God loved her and he heard her cries. He blessed her with two sons to bring forth a nation just for him. He blessed Leah even in her messed up family to produce a kingdom that would come to know him and love him. God is freeing her and he will free you too.

I need freedom

We as children of God cannot be blessed if we use the devil's ways to be blessed. We cannot truly receive from God what it is he wants to give us. He wants us to be free and not bound to this world. In John 8: verses 32 and 36 tell us the following:

"And ye shall know the truth, and the truth shall make you free."

"If the Son therefore shall make you free, ye shall be free indeed."

God wants us freed. He does not want us to die in the sin (flesh) that we are born into. In John 3 Jesus tells Nicodemus that a man must be born again. In 3:5-6 it says,

5"Jesus answered verily, verily, I say unto thee, Except a man be born of water and of the Spirit, he cannot enter into the kingdom of God."

6That which is born of the flesh is flesh; and that which

I AM HATED IN THIS HOUSE

is born of the Spirit is spirit."

As children of God we must be born of the spirit. We must live our lives in the spirit. Yes we are in this world, but we are not of this world. We must begin to live our lives through the grace that is sufficient enough to keep us (2 Cor. 12:9). The grace will see us through the hard times in our life. We are not tempted more than we can handle (1 Cor. 12:13).

Leah and Rachel were in a fleshly war against each other. They did not mean to be there, but they were. They had a lying, deceitful marriage on both sides and now they have to live together forever. Leah was not honored in her married. She was not honored by her father as being his daughter. She should have been given in marriage to a man who would have loved her, not to the one that showed up to marry her sister. Jacob did not honor Leah as his wife. She was a burden maybe, but she was the mother of his children. She deserved respect for that. He should not have treated her that way.

5

I Need A Companion

Genesis 29:34

And she conceived again, and bare a son; and said, Now this time will my husband be joined unto me, because I have born him three sons: therefore was his name called Levi.

Poor Leah. She is still trying to make Jacob love her. Poor us. We are still trying to make Michael, Phil or Johnny love us. I can not say this enough. A man will not love you because you had his baby. Please learn from Leah.

As God's daughters, we have to stop trying to convince a man to love us and learn to love ourselves. We spend so much time trying to get a man to look at us. Next we pray that they will like us. And after that if we are lucky enough he will love us. We have truly forgotten just who we are.

Who's child are you?

Rachel was gorgeous. She was beautiful according to the Bible (Gen.29:17). Jacob fell for her immediately. Leah was not attractive. She had an eye disorder, which worked against her for all of her life. Tricking Jacob into marrying her was a way for her father to secure her a husband and a home which he knew she would not be able to do on her own.

Rachel may have been favored by man, but Leah was favored by God. She was hated by man but was love of God. God will turn what was meant for evil into good. In Romans 8:28 it says, **"And we know that all things work together for good to them that love God, to them who are the called according to his purpose."**

Leah had a call. She was chosen. However, she did not know this and probably did not realize it until all her children were grown. God knew his purpose for her and how it would work out for her good.

Leah was trying to use the fact that she had three boys with Jacob as a way of receiving companionship from him. Funny part is, her third son's name is Levi which means companion.

Sidebar: *The tribe of Levi would become the tribe which the priests for God's tabernacle would come from. Truly, they were a companion, not to man, but to God for man.*

Leah was trying to, in a way, buy his love. We as women have to understand that we can have as many kids as we want for a man, but it is not going to make him love us. Love from a man must and has to come from him without strings attached.

I will take care of it for you

The woman's position in or society has changed. We are no longer only wives and mothers. We are not just secretaries or nurses. We are now more than 50% of the head of households (by choice or not). We are a great part of the workforce. We have risen up to the glass ceiling and cracked the glass in certain areas.

With everything we have done we are still trying to get men to love us by giving them stuff. We pay bills, car notices (sometimes buy cars or at least co-sign) pay bail and child support for his kids (that are not yours) or even paying rent for his apartment. We are hoping that he will love us for all the money oh, I am sorry, I mean the love we are showing him. Do you realize that you have a sign on your forehead that says ATM (Attracts Tired Men)?

Leah wanted her sons to do want they couldn't. She wanted them to produce the love from her husband towards her that she wanted and couldn't get from Jacob on her own. Some of us feel if we have children that it will make him love us. Why? Do you really believe a new born has the power to make another person love you? They cannot even feed themselves yet they will somehow convince a man to love you. You plot and scheme on how to make this happen only to have him leave you for another woman and she may become the wife you desired to be.

Or worse you use your children as pawns to hurt him because he may not love you, but he loves his children. You tell him that the only way he can see his kids is to be with you. You plot on how nice you will be when he comes to the house to pick up the kids. The end result you scheme for is him having sex with you. And when he does not fall for your tricks, you want to take him to court for child support (which should have happened before) or you are try to fight him or the new woman in his life. You tell the kids their daddy is nothing and he never wanted them. You know God is not pleased. This is not of God. God will repay, oh yes, he will. Read Deuteronomy 7:9-10.

Sidebar: Stop it.

How do I look?

If we are not trying to buy stuff or have kids by a man who only likes us, not loves us, we are destructing our bodies to look like someone who does not exist. I cannot believe women have been having plastic surgery to look like a doll. A plastic baby doll at that. We have become such a lustful society. The television has become a teaching tool to our daughters teaching them that if they are not a blonde size 8 and have a 36 DD breasts with a 28-inch waist, they are nobody. That is crazy. We are not all going to be blonde or a size 8 or 36DD with a 28-inch waist. God did not creature us all the same. The one time when man thought he would like to be like God he became knowledgeable of good and evil and we fell.

The sin of changing the image of God (plastic surgery) is idolatry and God hates idolatry more than everything else. If you read the first few commandments, they speak on idol worship. No worship of other gods. You can make yourself your own god. Did you know that?

In Proverbs 23:7 it says, **"For as he thinketh in his heart so is he:"** If you believe you are not pretty enough, smart enough or talented enough according to the world's standards stop that stinking thinking. This is a stronghold that has to be destroyed. This stronghold is in the mind and it will steal your dreams and destroy your image of yourself and kill your faith in God about his promises toward you. There are two beings that want to be your companion. They both want to fellowship with you. They are the devil and Jesus. Now, you cannot serve both and they both cannot reside in the same place. They need your full attention. We are talking about these two men and what their missions are in depth.

The Devil

The devil is a large part of this story. He is a big part of our story as well. He has been around for a long time. In scripture, we see that the devil is called a liar and the father of lies John 8:44 **"Ye are of your father the devil, and the lusts of your father ye will do. He was a murderer from the beginning, and abode not in the truth, because there is no truth in him. When he speaketh a lie, he speaketh of his own: for he is a liar, and the father of it."**

The devil is a liar and constantly tells them. He lies to us about everything. The way we were, the way we are and what the future holds. He has a problem with our Father and he will try anything to make our lives a living hell. His final destination is the pit of hell and he is trying to take as many of us there with him as he can. In the book of Isaiah chapter 14, there we see the relationship that Lucifer (Satan, Devil) had with God.

[12]How art thou fallen from heaven, O Lucifer, son of the morning! How art thou cut down to the ground, which didst weaken the nations!

[13]For thou hast said in thine heart, I will ascend into heaven, I will exalt my throne above the stars of God: I will sit also upon the mount of the congregation, in the

sides of the north:

¹⁴I will ascend above the heights of the clouds; I will be like the most High,

¹⁵Yet thou shalt be brought down to hell, to the sides of the pit.

Satan was in heaven. He was the son of the morning. He fell because he wanted to be above God. He thought (remember that word thought) he could just take over heaven and rule. God was not going to allow a created being to take over the creator. This would have been crazy. When God learned of this, he kicked Lucifer and one-third of the angels in heaven out and they were all doomed to hell. I am pretty sure there are some who regret making the decision to be on Lucifer's side. They'd probably would like to go back in time and change their minds. The devil was kicked out of heaven and doomed to roam the second heaven until his casting into the pit of hell. He is now going to and fro in the earth trying to build as many strongholds in our mind as he can.

Now, you may be asking yourself, what is a stronghold. A stronghold according to the dictionary is a fortified place or a fortress and major centre or area of predominance. (3) Our mind is a major centre. Our mind stores our thought, perceptions, and images, of and about ourselves. This is where we store all the good and bad thoughts about ourselves. They are first told to us when we are children by our family members. Then we hear from our peers (friends and enemies in our childhood) and people in authority (teachers, pastors neighbors, doctors). Then we have the television which is constantly putting bad images before our faces and placing thoughts (strongholds) of doubt about who we are and what we stand for.

The initial stronghold against men can be found in the first book of the Bible. In Genesis 3 Satan convinces woman that if she ate the fruit from the tree of life that she would not die, but they would become as gods. She and Adam thought (stronghold) on it and then ate and changed the world that was to come because they acted on a thought. Satan cannot make you do anything, but he can get you to think about things. We have to be very careful about what we think. Scripture tells us in Philippians 4:8 **"Finally, brethren, whatsoever things are true, whatsoever things are honest, whatsoever things are just, whatsoever things are pure, whatsoever things are lovely, whatsoever things are of good report; if there be any virtue, and if there be any praise, think on these things."**

Our actions are dictated by our mind. As I have stated before in Proverbs 23:7 **"For as he thinketh in his heart, so is he."** We are what we think we are.

What is on your mind?

If you think you will not amount to anything, then you won't. On the contrary, if you think you are somebody, then you are. Your thoughts, not what others think of you, makes you turn a noun into a verb. Here is an example of turning a noun into a verb in the negative sense. Example: Someone tells you that you are stupid. If you take in what they say and process it, you will begin to behave in a 'stupid' manner and thus you become it. That's taking a noun and turning it into a verb. Once you begin acting out what the person has called you, even if you don't remember them saying it to you, the verb has become an action in motion.

The devil will suggest things to us that only we can do. The devil cannot make you do anything he can only suggest. As he did with the woman and Adam, he does the same with us. He is limited in what he can do to us. When Jesus came down from heaven, he came to bring us something. Something that we could not and would not be able to do on our own. In John 10:10 is the scripture that will bring knowledge, wisdom and understanding.

John 10:10: **'The thief cometh not, but for to steal, and to kill, and to destroy: I am come that they might have life, and that they might have it more abundantly."**

Let's break this down

The thief (the devil) cometh not but to steal (to take or get something secretly, surreptitiously, or through trickery) (4) and to kill (to destroy or severely damage an essential, often delicate quality in something by superimposing something stronger) (5) and to destroy (to ruin something or make something useless) (6). Let's take a closer look at the first part of this scripture. It is

I NEED A COMPANION

important that we pay attention to what Jesus said.

Jesus informs us that there is a thief. He calls the devil a thief. He knows exactly who the devil is and what he wants. The thief comes to steal. He is coming to take something from you. He is going to do this through trickery. He will try to take our mind (the center of consciousness that generates thoughts, feelings, ideas, and perceptions, and stores knowledge and memories) (7). He is after the part of us that can separate us from God. We cannot allow the thief to steal the thoughts that we should be thinking on (Remember Phil.4:8).

If he can get you to think about the bad thoughts or ideas and feelings (because as women we live by your feelings), he has the power to kill (superimpose something stronger). He now has a stronghold in your mind. He is able to kill your thoughts that would help us to grow stronger in Christ. It will stop you from learning the wisdom of God through his word. If you learn that the word is true and it is living and will change you from the inside out, the thief cannot get any glory from that. He wants to keep you feeling the same way you did when your father told you that you were his little fat dumpling. You now see this as insult, but it really was his way of say something sweet to you. The devil now has a stronghold. He lives for this. If he can destroy (make useless) your thoughts of good report, he has you.

He did this to Leah. He put a stronghold and was stealing her thoughts. He told her she was not pretty enough to get her own husband. She was killed in her thoughts that she could have

Jacobs's baby and that it would make him love her. He was able to make her thoughts useless and convince her that if she had a few more babies, he would stop loving her sister and be her true love. Yes, she prayed to God, but she did not believe what she was praying for. She was praying amiss. James tells us in James 4:3 that **"Ye ask, and receive not, because ye ask amiss, that ye may consume it upon your lusts:"** Leah prayed that God would help her in her marriage, but really she wanted Jacob to love her like he loved her sister Rachel. When we are so focused on getting someone or something for our own selfish means God my give us what we want, but it will never be what we want it to be. Leah does not get Jacob to love her even after four kids (and never does). She has asked God in and for her own lust.

Now we have a better understanding of the first companion, the devil.

Sidebar: The devil is the first because he is the your Flesh. Jesus is the second in this text because he came as the second Adam to redeem man back to God.

Now let us get an understanding of the second companion, Jesus.

Jesus

Jesus also has a purpose. His purpose is in the second part of the verse John 10:10 which says, **"I am come that they might have life, and that they might have it more abundantly."** Jesus came to give us something. It is life. What is life? The meaning that I liked is the following: the character or conditions of somebody's existence (8). Jesus came to improve our existence. He came to improve our conditions. Which conditions of our lives did Jesus come to improve? Phil. 4:19 states: **"But my God shall supply all your need according to his riches in glory by Christ Jesus."** Jesus will not only take care of your spiritual needs but, also our physical and financial needs. There are no conditions we have that he will not take care of. In Psalms 132:15 God says, **"I will abundantly bless her provision."** Jesus sees and deals with your needs beforehand. Your blessing is coming and it will be abundant. We do not have to be fearful of what the devil may try. He is completely defeated. In Rev 1:18 Jesus stated clearly **"I am he that liveth, and was dead; and, behold, I am alive for evermore, Amen; and have the keys of hell and of death."** The devil has no power over us. He is a good persuader, but powerless.

Jesus needs something from us to be able to bless us. Can you guess what that is? He needs you just as you are. Incomplete, confused, lonely, scared, angry, frustrated and in need of love. He will take all of it, if you let him. Jesus wants to give you rest. Matt. 11:29 says, **"Take my yoke upon you, and learn of me; for I am meek and lowly in heart: and ye shall find rest unto your souls."** There is an important scripture before this one if you want rest. Matt 11:28 says, **"Come unto me, all ye that labour and are heavy laden, and I will give you rest."** Jesus makes it very clear what we have to do to find his rest. You must come to him. Stop right there. You must decide to live for him and him alone. You cannot be friends with the world and expect God to bless.

In James, 4:4 it says, **"Ye adulterers and adulteresses, know ye not that the friendship of the world is enmity with God? whosoever therefore will be a friend of the world is the enemy of God."** We cannot commit adultery with other gods (man, woman, jobs, positions, cars, homes, kids and anything that takes our worship off of God) and think God is going to allow this to happen. You have to pick a side. You have to come completely over. Once that is done, he will begin a work in you. You cannot labour this out yourself. You are too burdened down. How could you? The Holy Spirit will come in and become your Comforter. Jesus says so. In John 15:26 he says, **"But when the Comforter (Counselor, Helper, Advocate, Intercessor, Strengthener, Standby) comes, Whom I will send to you from the Father, the Spirit of Truth Who comes (proceeds) from the Father, He [Himself] will testify regarding Me (AMP)."**

You cannot be transformed without the transformer. You cannot have comfort with the Comforter. He is the Spirit of God. You need him to dwell in you. You need him to help you to fight the good fight of faith. This walk is not easy, but it is worth it. The major fight you will constantly have will be in our mind. The devil would love to have your mind. The mind is where we have free will. The mind is where our little gods live. The mind is where we discern good and evil.

Scripture tells us that we have to renew our minds. In

Ephesians 4:23 **"And be renewed in the spirit of your mind;"** We are two spirits, one good and one evil. Don't let anybody tell you the devil will leave you alone now that you have accepted Jesus. That is a lie from the pit. Our true fight begins then. The devil is mad and wants you back. We have to renew our good spirit daily. We have to pray, read, mediate, listen to Godly word and then begin to live what we have read and heard. In James 1:22 says, **"But be ye doers of the word, and not hearers only, deceiving your own selves."** We cannot keep going to church for years and never grow. This is not God. We have to work out our salvation. In Phil. 2:12 **"Wherefore, my beloved, as ye have always obeyed, not as in my presence only, but now much more in my absence, work out your own salvation with fear and trembling."** Salvation does not end with the sinner's prayer. It begins there. You now have the same death as Jesus. You need to hang the shame, sorrow, hurt, pain and disappointment on the cross and leave it there. Jesus did. Jesus died on the cross and bore every sin that every man has ever committed and would commit to free us from the bondage of this present world. Once we are with Christ, we are no longer tied to this world, but we are aliens just passing through. We have to begin to mind the things of God and not this world. We have to die daily. In 1 Cor. 15:31 **"Protest by your rejoicing which I have in Christ Jesus our Lord, I die daily."** We like Paul must learn to die daily. We must constantly crucify the flesh.

We have to transform. Romans 12:2 **"And be not conformed to this world: but be ye transformed by the renewing of your mind, that ye may prove what is that**

good, and acceptable, and perfect, will of God." As our minds are transforming we will begin to change the impure thoughts and ideas we once had. We will begin to see that God's will is flawless and if we learn his ways and how he really thinks about us, we will become perfect and acceptable in his will for us. What is meant for me is not meant for you, but it is still in the perfect will of God. Our God is not a baker, but a potter. We are his clay. He makes us all different. We come with different gifts and callings. He will mold us into what will serve his purpose for our lives and make it a life worth living. He cannot make us all the same because it's not what he wants. God loves difference. If you do not believe me just looks around. You will not find two people that are the same. You can see twins, but they will have some differences, whether in looks or behavior. Jesus is looking for a transformation of your mind. He needs you to learn that it is really a choice you have to make. You have to want to change. You have to believe in him. You need to have faith. In Hebrews 12:1 says, **"Now faith is the substance of things hope for, the evidence of things not seen."** What are you hoping for? There is nothing in life you cannot have if you can hope for it. When we were kids we could hope for things without a problem. We would trust in our mothers and fathers to give us what they said they would. I know that my son trust me to keep my promises to him. Well we serve a God that not only keeps his promises, but is well able to do so. Paul cannot have said this better **"Now unto him that is able to do exceeding abundantly above all that we ask or think, according to the power that worketh in us,"**

Your hope will move your faith. If you do not have hope,

you have no faith. You cannot say I believe in God and do not hope that he will bring you out of your trials. You cannot do it, remember you tried. Your man, he tried, it did not work. Your mother and father cannot do it, they tried it and did not work. There is only one person who can work it out and not just work it out, but do exceeding abundantly above all. Who else can do it but God? He is above all. You cannot think of all his blessings. You cannot measure them. You cannot begin to count them. You were blessed before you came to him. He kept you. When the devil wanted to kill you or have you kill yourself, God was with you. The power that works in you is the Holy Spirit. He can only do what Jesus commands. He will only work that which is for the good. In Rom. 8:28 states **"And we know that all things work together for good to them that love God, to them who are the called according to his purpose."** Are you hoping for money, a man, kids, a good job or a new home of your own? Are you hoping for peace of mind, joy in the trials and patience in the valley? Can you see the blessing? Can you live without seeing where it is coming from? Can you hope without the eye candy? Can you trust God without some man showing you the way? Can you love you in spite of you? Do you have the faith to know that God comes to make your life abundant? If you do, then this scripture should bring some praise. Psalm 145:7 **"They shall abundantly utter the memory of thy great goodness, and shall sing of thy righteousness."** We should never forget where God has brought us from. We all have a story. This is our testimony. They come with different story lines, plot and dramas, but they all end with us coming to the one that can save everyone. Jesus!

6

God Is My Praise

Genesis 29:35

And she conceived again, and bare a son: and she said, Now will I praise the LORD: therefore she called his name Judah; and left bearing.

I have a testimony

Sidebar: If I were to bring Leah up to our time, I believe she would be going to church. She would testify about this wonderful change that has happened in her life.

Leah had the moment that changed her life. Leah realized that she had a testimony. She started believing God and stopped believing her family. As she was on her way to church, she began to look back over her life. God blessed her with four boys. That is a strong family right there. Four boys mean the legacy will continue. She has a legacy. Having a legacy wasn't supposed to happen for her. As she enters the doors of the church, she hears Psalms 100:4 **"Enter into his gates with thanksgiving, and into his courts with praise: be thankful unto him, and bless his name."** She was told she wasn't pretty enough. That devil lied. She will have grandchildren and people who would love of her. A family that would take care of her. Leah's father spoke a curse into her life, but God blessed her. She would have raised her hand during the testimony part of the service. Her testimony would be: "I now have a life that is abundant. I know God was with me. In Psalms 100:3 **"Know ye that the LORD he is God: it is he that hath made us, and not we ourselves; we are his people, and the sheep of his pasture."**

She would testify of how she was afflicted in her house and how God brought her joy. She was hated, but God brought her love. She needed a companion and God became her friend. After her testimony, Leah finally reached her praise place.

Come on and Praise him

We have to come to our praise place. We reach our praise place when we realize that God is all we need. He is our sole provider, protector and supporter. When we get this in our mind and believe this more than our feelings, we have are in our praise place. We need a place to praise him. This place is just God and you. No kids, husband, family or friends. No outside distractions. No flesh can be there. You have to be free to allow the Holy Spirit to have free will in your life. You need a place that will allow you to give God praise for all he has done for you. You will not need to have a physical praise place just a mental place. You will begin to praise God mentally for what he has done. Allow the Spirit of God to begin to worship with you. The Holy Spirit knows how to worship. He will worship with moaning and groaning, if you do not have the words to say. Then you will become verbal with your praise. Speak Your Praise. Speak your joy. Speak your pain. Speak your hurt. You need to praise God for all he has done. The morning sunshine, the bed you just slept in and for the water you just washed yourself with. The home you live in. The praise should continue throughout your day. Give him praise for the good and the bad. He knows what the outcome will be. Trust in his faithfulness over your life. Do not trust in your eyes, ears or flesh, but trust God's word it is true.

The word of God is truth and in them you will find life. Praise scriptures are throughout the bible. I was able to find 259 verses that had the word praise in them. It starts from Genesis to Revelations. I will just give you a few.

I HAVE MY PRAISE

Deuteronomy 10:21 **"He is thy praise, and he is thy God, that hath done for thee these great and terrible things, which thine eyes have seen. "**

What has God shown you that you should praise him for?

Deuteronomy 26:19 **"And to make thee high above all nations which he hath made, in praise, and in name, and in honour; and that thou mayest be an holy people unto the LORD thy God, as he hath spoken."**

Has God promoted you? You better praise him.

1 Chronicles 16:25: **"For great is the LORD, and greatly to be praised: he also is to be feared above all gods."**

Your God is above all other gods. Praise him.

2 Samuel 22:4 **"I will call on the LORD, who is worthy to be praised: so shall I be saved from mine enemies."**

Has the Lord saved you from your enemies? Give him some glory. Hallelujah.

Psalms 7:17 **"I will praise the LORD according to his righteousness: and will sing praise to the name of the LORD most high."**

What is your praise song? I know I have one.

Psalms 22:26 'the meek shall eat and be satisfied: they shall praise the LORD that seek him: your heart shall live forever.'

Are you meek and satisfied?

Psalms 145:2 **"Every day will I bless thee; and I will praise thy name for ever and ever"**

Have you praised God today for his many blessings?

Daniel 4:37 **"Now I Nebuchadnezzar praise and extol and honour the King of heaven, all whose works are truth, and his ways judgment: and those that walk in pride he is able to abase."**

Has your enemy praised your God for the things he has seen your God do for you on your behalf?

1 Peter 2:9 **"But ye are a chosen generation, a royal priesthood, an holy nation, a peculiar people; that ye should shew forth the praises of him who hath called you out of darkness into his marvelous light;"**

Praise God for who you are and what he has called you out of. We have to get into the habit of giving him praise (the extolling of a deity or the rendering of homage and gratitude to a deity) (9) . Praising God is a daily habit we need to have. Thank him for what he has done. Leah did.

I HAVE MY PRAISE

She named her fourth son Judah which means praise. He may have been born fourth, but he was moved to first. God loves praise. Judah was the tribe that led the children of Israel with praise and worship. They were the praise tribe. You must praise God before the battle in order to get the victory. They did this at the walls of Jericho. Please read Joshua chapter 6. The children of Israel had victory because they were obedient and gave God praise. Praise first, then you will have victory over your enemies.

Leah began to worship God for all the things she was told she would not have. She thanked God for the things he had already done on her behalf. God inhabits the praises of his people. In Psalms 22:3 it says, **"But thou art holy, O thou that inhabitest the praises of Israel."** When you praise him, he will come in. God will show up and show out on our behalf. He will change the atmosphere for you to have a life that is abundant. If you spend your time praising, worshiping or thanking God, you will not have time to get caught up into thinking bad thoughts. Keep your mind stayed on God. Isaiah 26:3 says, **"Thou wilt keep him in perfect peace, whose mind is stayed on thee: because he trusteth in thee."** Where is your peace? Is your peace tied to someone other than God? Man cannot give you the peace that you need. God's peace passes all understanding. The scripture Phil. 4:7 says, **"And the peace of God, which passeth all understanding, shall keep your hearts and minds through Christ Jesus."** When we stay focused on the purpose that God has for your lives' we will become the daughters whom he has made us to be. We will be free. Jesus came to free us. In John 8:37 Jesus tells us that **"If the Son therefore shall**

make you free, ye shall be free indeed." Well, if you have the Son, then you are liberated and not just released but freed indeed. You are guaranteed freedom from the things of this world. When you have freedom, you can now live abundantly. God never intended for us to live in fear, but to live victorious. We need to trust God that he will do all to protect us from all the snares of the devil.

Leah's praise brought about change. When we praise God, there will be a change. You cannot stay in the same mindset once you begin to praise him. The praise and worship will turn into devotion. Then you will want to do God's will for your life. The devil cannot and will not stay in the presence of a praise session to God. He hates that. Satan wants to be praised. If he can get you to think that you do not have to give God any praise he has won. He does not mind you wanting to read the bible. He will just criticize God that he has help someone else, but not you. He does not mind you wanting to go to church because you can walk in with him and leave with him the same way. You are in church planning what you want you to do when you leave church. Where should I eat? What time is this service going to be over? Or maybe you have anger toward someone in the church. You are sitting in church with a frown on your face because sister so-so made you mad. You cannot praise God because you have not forgiven them. God cannot be praised properly when you have unforgivingness in your heart. Jesus was very clear when he said in Matt 18:35 that **"So likewise shall my heavenly Father do also unto you, if ye from your hearts forgive not everyone his brother their trespasses."** Remember you cannot expect a blessing when you are a burden to your brother. The devil does not mind you watching Christian TV shows because he knows that you are only getting a piece of God's word. This will make you weak and easy for him to steal your praise thoughts. Please read Matt. 18:18-23, Jesus' parable about the sower.

How is your soil? Is the seed (words of God) growing? Are you sitting in front of the TV not learning about your new life? You need a house of worship to get some water and have your soil cultivated.

Like Leah, we have to get pass the pain from our families, friends, and even people in the church. We have to let go of the unforgivingness that is stopping us from growing in the word of God and towards him. We have to accept ourselves just the way we are: broken, hurting and afraid of everything and everybody and then give it to God. He will heal, mend and fix all the broken pieces of our heart. You will have nothing to do with things, but it will be about your soul healing. It will be about your journey becoming brighter and easier. Your praise will become your life. And how wonderful will that be?

Epilogue

Isaiah 65:1-3

¹I WAS [ready to be] inquired of by those who asked not; I was [ready to be] found by those who sought Me not. I said, Here I am, here I am [says I AM] to a nation [Israel] that has not called on My name.

²I have spread out My hands all the day long to a rebellious people, who walk in a way that is not good, after their own thoughts

³A people who provoke Me to My face continually, sacrificing [to idols] in gardens and burning incense upon bricks [instead of at God's prescribed altar];

God is waiting

As we come to the end of our journey reading about Leah's testimony, I would like to leave you with something. God desires a relationship with us, but we keep saying NO. Every time you say I cannot or I could not you are telling God NO. Every time God tells you to go right and you go left you are telling him NO. Every time you pray for something and then turn around and not believe God for it, but doubt the outcome because you believe that it is taking too long, you are telling God NO.

God is in heaven waiting for us to come to him according to the scriptures in Isaiah 65:1-3. Can you imagine God waiting for you to just talk to him? He is crying out to you to all of us and we constantly provoke him with our daily worship of other gods (car, house, kids, jobs, money, husband or wife and positions). He desires our attention and we will not give it to him. We ignore him to go following our own mind's desires. We seek after the corruptible thing instead of the incorruptible. God is incorruptible. He is the only person in the world that will wait for us to turn to him and seek him. He loves us so much. God is in heaven waiting and calling out for you. Can you imagine that?

Trust Him

We need to learn to trust God. He is our total source. When Leah began to trust God that is when she could praise him. If you would like to praise him, trust God. Trust him with your life. He created you, why can't we trust him to take care of us? David says it best in Psalm 56:4 **"In God, I will praise his word, in God, I have put my trust; I will not fear what flesh can do unto me."**

Why are we so fearful of flesh? Man cannot do anything to us unless God says so. As he was with Job so is he with us. God allowed all things. He is with us at all times. I Peter 3:12 says, **"For the eyes of the Lord are over the righteous, and his ears are open unto their prayers."** God is constantly watching over us. He looks out for us even we do not look out for ourselves. He loves and he hears our prayers. Not some of them and not a part of them, but all. He will answer them if we trust him to do so.

<u>God is watching you.</u>

2 Chron. 16:9 **"For the eyes of the LORD run to and fro throughout the whole earth, to shew himself strong in the behalf of them whose heart is perfect toward him"**

God is constantly looking for ways to show himself on our behalf. He is working towards a perfect marriage between his bride and himself. Is your heart perfect towards him? Are you still holding on to things he is trying to get you to let go of? God throws our sins into the deep of the sea and we go get a row boat and some scuba gear and oxygen tanks. We then travel all the way there and swim down to the ocean floor to pick them up again. Every time you allow the thief to keep a bad thought running around in your mind instead of resisting him, you have picked it back up again and you are telling God No you cannot hold this.

Sidebar I have two words for you STOP IT.

<u>Your gift is before you</u>

Proverbs 18:16 "A man's gift maketh room for him, and bringeth him before great men."

There is a gift that God has given you. Yes we all have gifts that are given without repentance according to Romans 11:29.

God will make room for that gift in your life to show his glory. He will cause that gift to have you in places of high esteem and doing things you never dreamed you could do. As with Leah, she could not see the wonderful future she would have, but God made room for her gift. Never worry about man, only be concerned about doing God's will with your life. He will make room for you.

Prayer for God's Daughters

My prayer is that this book has been a help to you in knowing your worth in God. You are not what others may have said you are. You are a child of the most high God and you have the kingdom in you.

Maybe you are reading this book and you do not know Jesus as your Lord and Savior. You can invite him in right now. Just recite this prayer:

Dear Father,
I surrender to you as of today. I am a sinner and need you. I believe that Jesus came down from heaven and shed his blood and died for me. I believe that he rose on the third day and I am asking you to come into heart and life as my personal Lord and Savior. To guide and directed my life from now on. I ask this in the name of Jesus, Amen.

Maybe you know Jesus, but you have walked away and want the relationship back the way it was. God desires for his children to return back home. As the father did with his prodigal son, God will do to you. You can pray now to be restored. He never left you.

Dear Father,
I am coming back to you. I know that I have walked away from you, but right now I am asking to come home. I know that you can and will restore me. I thank you right now, in the name of Jesus. Amen

I believe that whatever you want from God he is going to perform it as long as it is in line with his purpose for you. God is not a man that he would lie and not the son of man that he should repent.

Reference Notes

All the bible verses are from the King James Version or unless otherwise stated. The others are from the Amplified bible.

Destination- from free dictionary .com
Talebearer- from merriam-webster free dictionary .com
Stronghold-from dictionary.com
Steal- from freedictionary.com
Kill-from freedictionary.com
Destroy- from free dictionary.com
Mind- from freedictionary.com
Life- from freedictionary.com
Praise-from freedictionary.com

About The Author

Cynthia Robinson was born on November 10, 1967 in Newark, New Jersey where she still resides with her husband Victor. Cynthia is the proud mother of six children. Cynthia was an hotelier by trade before her call to ministry to be a helper of women. She was ordained an Evangelist in 2010 by her Pastor, Barbara Glanton, at The Love of Jesus Family Church in Newark, New Jersey. Recently, Cynthia was appointed to head the Women Support Ministry at her church.

Cynthia is the founder of God's Daughters Ministry. The ministry is found on the belief that all of God's Daughters need to receive enlightenment, be encouraged and empowered in order for the seven pillars of a woman to be standing. The seven pillars are Spiritual, Emotional, Mental, Physical, Financial, Verbal and Sexual. When these areas are strengthened by the word of God then the ministry foundational scripture in Proverbs 14: 1 will be easy to accomplish **"Every wise woman buildeth her house: but the foolish plucketh it down with her hands."**

'I am Leah' is Cynthia Robinson first book. It is about the destructive similarities all women have to face on a daily basis that can and will be a hinderance to their growth in God if we do not allow God's word to direct us into our true purpose .

If you would like to have Evangelist Cynthia Robinson come and speak at your church, retreat or women's conference please email her at cyntrob01@yahoo.com.She is a woman of God that is willing to help all her sisters make heaven their home.

Order Form

Evangelist Cynthia Robinson
cyntrob01@yahoo.com
www.iamleah.org

Name _____

Address _____

City/State/Zip _____

Phone _____

email _____

Quantity _____ @ $10.00 each

Shipping Cost: $4.00 for the first book and $1.00 for each additional book.